VOLMANIA

...AY GOD CREATED"

RA
1992

ANOTHER VOL
VICTORY SECURED

Chelsea Kirkpatrick takes
advantage of a slumber
party with 107,000 of her
closest friends on a
Saturday afternoon in
Knoxville.

VOLMANIA

Shannon Parks Williams

Photography by
Harrison McClary

ART DIRECTION   Shannon Parks Williams/Mike Goodson

DESIGN   Mike Goodson, The Goodson Group, Nashville, TN

BINDING   BindTech, Inc., Nashville, TN

PRINTING   Harris Press, Nashville, TN

AREA
RESTRICTED TO
ORANGE

Enemies beware:
these Vol fans
mean business.

Sports Mania Productions, LLC
917 Mt Pleasant Road
Kingston Springs, TN 37082

PREFACE

When I started out to write this book I really had no idea how much I would learn to love Tennessee football. The tradition. The pageantry. The excitement that builds as the Pride of the Southland Band lines up in "T" formation minutes before kick-off. It's an exhilarating feeling and one that I never would have known had it not been for my husband, Matt Williams. This book is dedicated proudly to him.

One Saturday afternoon three years ago, when we had only been dating for a little while, Matt came to my condominium as I was in the middle of housework. He offered to vacuum for me, and upon opening my hall closet, noticed a fur coat that was the color of Tennessee orange. I didn't know it then, but after that day he told all of his friends he had found the girl he was going to marry. The coat now belongs to Sally Langley, one of the biggest UT fans alive, but the memory will always remain.

We started going to games and one thing led to another. Before I knew it I was a fan and, as I looked around me, I realized that someone should do a book about all of us crazy people. So I elected myself to do the job.

There are so many wonderful people to thank for their support. You all know who you are, but in case you don't, I'll name just a few: Tonny and Ireene Vanderleeden, Jim and Brenda Williams, Janis Christenson, Les and Glenda Acree, Greg and Sally Langley, Bubba Miller, Stephen Linn, Mike Goodson (for everything), David Bohan, Pat Williams, Steve and Susie Mathews, William S. Parks, M.D., and most of all, Harrison McClary.

I hope you enjoy this book as much as I did making it.

GO BIG O!

Shannon Parks Williams
August, 1998

INTRODUCTION

Great games, plays, players and coaches have come and gone in the more than 100 years of University of Tennessee football. Perhaps the only facet of Tennessee football more consistent than the teams' on the field performances is the outpouring of support of Volunteer football fans as nearby as Oak Ridge and stretching across the country.

Volmaniacs will tell you about some of the great things about Tennessee football:

- A 40-18 drubbing of Notre Dame in 1979.

- Shocking #1 ranked Auburn and Heisman winner Bo Jackson in 1985.

- A Sugar Bowl humbling of a Miami Hurricane team led by another Heisman named Vinny.

- 1991's "Miracle at South Bend": a 35-34 comeback on Notre Dame's home field.

- Capping the 1997 season as SEC Champions with a victory over SEC rival Auburn.

All truly great moments in Tennessee football, any Volmaniac will tell you. They'll also tell you about the excitement that builds inside from the commencement of summer until the Vols first game. They'll tell you they prefer listening to John Ward no matter who is calling the game. Bragging about a closet filled with orange apparel is a proud moment for any Volmaniac. They'll tell you they don't sleep before the Florida game. They'll tell you Jerry Colquitt's knee injury in the 1994 opener was outright cruel. They'll tell you about the lump in their throat the last time Peyton ran through the 'T.' They'll tell you that it's hard to beat being on The Hill on a Saturday in the fall. And they'll tell you

IT'S GREAT TO BE A TENNESSEE VOL!

Meet the stories, the places and most importantly the fans that make up

VOLMANIA.

FORWARD

In the 31 years that I have been the Public Address Announcer for the University of Tennessee football games, I have been witness to the antics of some of the most rabid Volmaniacs. I have seen them on the field and off, have enjoyed many of their tailgate parties and have even been inside a few of their homes. But not until now have I seen them encapsulated in a book. With that thought in mind, it gives me great pleasure to announce VOLMANIA, the book.

I first heard about this project a few months ago when I was introduced to the book's creator, Shannon Williams, who was seeking my advice. Her idea immediately struck a chord with me, because it was different than all of the many books on the University of Tennessee football program that had come before. Instead of dealing with the great plays, players and coaches that have come and gone through the team's rich history, VOLMANIA deals with the fans of the football program who make cheering for the Vols as exciting as it is.

VOLMANIA is the first book that deals solely with the fans of the Volunteers, not only how they come to the games but how they *live*. From Tennessee's own flotilla, the Vol Navy, to the home of Sally Langley (who, with her sister Sandy Troop are known to UT fans everywhere as "The Twins"), this book focuses on the folks who take the word "hobby" one step further, showing their colors in the true sense of the word.

If you are a University of Tennessee football fan, or just a fan of rich heritage and tradition, then VOLMANIA is a must for your collection.

Welcome to VOLMANIA!

—Bobby Denton
Vice President/General Manager
Dick Broadcasting/WIVK Radio, flagship station of the Tennessee Volunteers

VOL WALK

Big Orange Fans line Volunteer Boulevard
to offer some last words of encouragement
to the players as they make their way from
Gibbs Hall to Neyland Stadium.

"I'll never forget the feeling of that last Vol Walk
heading towards the Vanderbilt Game."

Coach Phillip Fulmer, 1997

GAME DAY

"In the East college football is a cultural exercise. On the West Coast it is a tourist attraction. In the Midwest it is cannibalism. But in the Deep South it is religion, and Saturday is the Holy Day."

Marino Casem
Former coach, Alcorn University

For many Tennesseans, Saturday is the middle of a three-day football extravaganza, beginning with Friday afternoon's pilgrimage to Knoxville and ending Sunday with a weary drive home. But there in the middle, on Saturday afternoon in and around Neyland Stadium, every football fan will tell you there isn't a place in Heaven or on Earth they'd rather be.

ONE LAST TIME

Volmaniacs turn out to see

#16 bid farewell.

"I got started by going to the Cotton Bowl in 1989. We won. Barely. I had gone to get a hot dog and by the time I got back, Tennessee had scored two touchdowns and I missed them both."

Frank Bender

Knoxville, Tennessee

"My father-in-law played on the '28 and '29 teams with Houston Herndon. I went to my first game in '47 and have been going ever since. Sometimes we drive all the way up to Knoxville and turn around and come right back. But we've always enjoyed UT football through the years. Win or lose, we still go."

Herbert Schilling
Father-in-law

FAMILY TRADITION

The Shelton family
(R to L) Robert, Robbie,
Melissa, and father-in-
law, Herbert Schilling

Humboldt, Tennessee

GETTING THERE

Tennessee football fans have long been recognized as being some of the most loyal followers of their team. Be it a short drive to Nashville or cross-country to Los Angeles, Vol fans will use bus, plane, boat, automobile, limousine, van, recreational vehicle, hearse or bicycle in Big Orange style to be where the Vols play on Saturday. For a traveling Vol fan, getting to the game in a well-decked-out "Vol Mobile," especially on enemy turf, is as much of the weekend as the game itself.

Big Orange Babe

Sally Langley sits atop her Honda Prelude, complete with permanent orange decals — "those aren't magnets you see on my car" — a personalized license plate which reads "UT 4 EVER" and customized orange neon underneath.

BIG ORANGE STRETCH

John "Thunder" Thornton
of Chattanooga, Tennessee,
rides to games in high style,
courtesy of his Lincoln
limousine, the second
orange limo to have been
in his possession. "My first
one was an old Cadillac
that I bought for five
thousand bucks. We
painted it orange and
white and took it to every
winning game of the '93
season. And the three
games we didn't take it to,
Tennessee lost. When I
found out we were
opening the '94 season in
Los Angeles, I decided it
was time for an upgrade.

It hasn't won every game,
but I think it has the
greatest football record of
any limousine in the whole
Southeast, maybe the
whole country."

JOHN THORNTON'S SABERLINER 80 JET

"Originally I had a partner who wouldn't let me paint it, so I waited until I bought him out. Then I painted her underbelly Big Orange and since then it's been going 30 knots faster! We've had a lot of fun on the plane. It goes to most of the away games, never with an empty seat. And it's real easy to find on the tarmac. Most private jets are white with little modest decals and then there sits my big punkin'."

THE TENNESSEE
TRAVELERS

Donnie and Patsy Bittle,
Knoxville, Tenn.
Jimmy and Bettie Burcham,
Columbia, Tenn.
Frank and Evelyn Bender,
Knoxville, Tenn.
Frank and Carol Armstrong,
Columbia, Tenn.
Ed and Mary Lou Griffin,
Knoxville, Tenn.

*"We met by parking in the same place on Neyland Drive. We
started getting to know each other and having cookouts together. Then we started traveling together to the away games and
it's been really fun. It's a great way to meet new people that
share the same interests we do."*

Mary Lou Griffin

Evelyn Bender, Mary Lou Griffin,
Bettie Burcham, and Frank Bender
plot their course.

Jimmy and Bettie Burcham of Columbia, Tennessee lead a caravan of Big Orange faithful to another game. "I have this rug in front of my refrigerator that plays 'Rocky Top,'" Bettie says, "so I can tell when Jimmy is getting into the food." Betty had a VW convertible painted orange and white, but now she has a white Jeep Cherokee decorated with a helmet on the hood, scads of magnetic stuff and streamers flying off the back. "I drive it to work and everywhere I go. Yes, ma'am. All year long."

JEEP CHER-O-'T'EE

White is a favorite color for many Vol fans, as it is the easiest color upon which they can create personalized, limited edition Vol Mobiles.

"T" FOR TWO

Frank and Carol Armstrong's prized picnic table was made by
Nashvillian Robert O. Kelley. The tickets embedded in the table
are from the first game after Neyland Stadium was enlarged to
become the largest college football stadium in the country. Above:
The Armstrong's directors chairs pay tribute to legendary Voice Of
The Vols, John Ward.

"It came from a brothel in North Knoxville called The Ponderosa. It was used for transportation until a guy I know bought it in 1980. I helped him work on it for ten years and finally, when his wife said either she or the car were leaving, I made a deal with him where I mowed his lawn for three years and I got it.

"There have been guys that have come to our tailgate parties and whisper that they remember the car from it's original owner but not to tell anybody. One guy said he borrowed the car to go to a bachelor party at his father's house and when he pulled up, his dad came out and said, 'boys, you been to the Ponderosa?'"

— John McElroy

John and Louella McElroy
Knoxville, Tennessee

VOLMOBILE

*"We've had it for 28 years. A funeral home
was going to junk it so we bought it on a
credit card and spent 10 times as much fixing
it up. In those days they used it as a hearse
and as an ambulance. If the patient
survived, they'd take him to the hospital. If
not, they'd go straight to the funeral home.*

Joe Beals, M.D.

Knoxville, Tennessee

"Everybody thinks of crazy things to do anymore, but back then it was really wild. Our friends all thought we were crazy, but they all wanted rides."

Dr. Beals
and his wife, Catherine

ISLE OF ORANGE

P.J.'s Marina

Maryville, Tennessee

Preceding Page

"I love it, this is the life. I wish I would have done it a long time ago."

Wayne Gregory at home
on his houseboat
Maryville, Tennessee

"It's so peaceful. In the evenings, as I do my paperwork on the couch, I can look out and watch the folks come through. Everybody that comes by has something to say about the boat. It's quite a conversation piece."

Path to Neyland

SAYING GRACE

Vol fans have a unique way

of counting their blessings.

If I would have thought about it, my little girl would have been Orange Anne. With the last name being White, Orange Anne just fits. It's all I've ever called her, all I ever will call her. She's my Orange Anne."

Cannonball and
granddaughter
'Orange Anne' White
Nashville, Tennessee

We have a little orange and white cart that we pull behind this so we can have a foursome. We've redone the cart a couple of times, but right now it's checkerboard like the end zone at Neyland Stadium. We take it to all of the UT golf tournaments. Used to pull it on an orange and white trailer, but someone stole it a year or so ago. I guess they were UT fans, too.

Cannonball White, owner

Nashville, Tennessee

"I've been a UT fan ever since I can remember. I don't see how anybody could live in Tennessee and not be a Tennessee fan. I love the state and I love the team. They're wonderful. Neyland Stadium is a whole different world. There's no place I'd rather be on a Saturday afternoon. I'd turn down heaven."

Cannonball White with son, Mike
Nashville, Tennessee

"When Tennessee got the invitation to be in the Orange Bowl, some of my friends called and said they wanted to charter a plane and fly down to Miami. I started out renting a 10-seater plane and by the time it was all said and done, it had grown to 60 seats. We landed at a private airport and had two buses that picked us up on the tarmac and delivered us to the front door of the stadium. After it was all over they picked us up, delivered us to the front door of the airplane and we were home in Nashville by 2:30 a.m."

Paul Pratt, Jr. and friends
Franklin, Tennessee

1990 Honda
Goldwing with
matching trailer

"We had it done about
three years ago by a guy in
Kentucky that paints
show cars. We love motor-
cycles and Tennessee so
we decided to combine our
two favorite things into
one. We drive it to all the
away games. We have
people from here to
California that see the
orange and white and
honk their horn — you
can't imagine how many
Tennessee fans there are
across this country.
— Zula Davis

Ron and Zula Davis
Maryville, Tennessee

ROCKY THE BULLDOG

Named after "Rocky
Top," Rocky was given to
Donnie Bittle by his wife
Patsy after UT beat
Georgia in '97. Of course,
Rocky owns a full
wardrobe of UT clothing
which he wears proudly
to all of the games —
home and away.

GAME FACES

Get-ups galore, Tennessee fans arrive by the hundreds of thousands eleven Saturdays each fall. Dress is casual, but orange.

No different than green on St. Patrick's or red on St. Valentine's, in Knoxville in the fall one wears orange. Not because it's necessarily fashionable (although that could be argued), donning oneself in head-to-toe orange provides an all-access pass to the best club in the US — Club Orange — and admission is free.

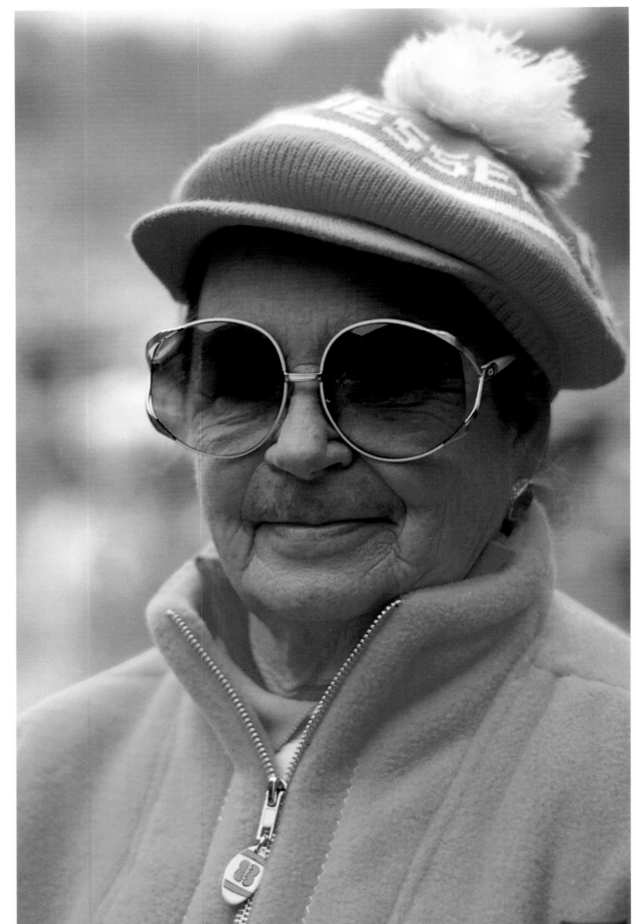

"I've been a Volunteer fan all my life and that's 67 years. I can remember back listening to every game on the radio until I finally got big enough to go. Since then, I haven't missed a-one."

Sue Henard
Bristol, Tennessee

GIVE 'EM SIX!

A Tennessee fan's

greatest moment.

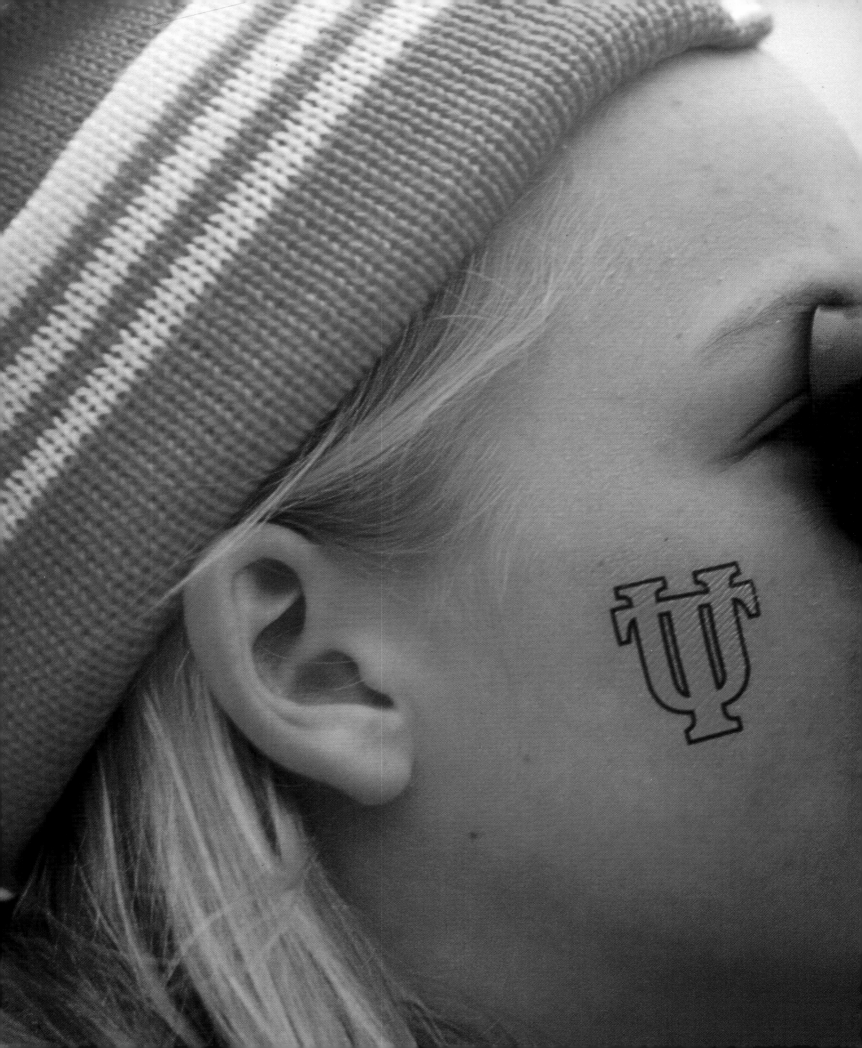

VOLAPALOOZA

The Burchams do it

up in anticipation of a

championship showdown

in Atlanta.

Anita Waldrop

a.k.a.

"Prissy the Clown"

Acworth, Georgia

85

HATS OFF

*"This is my lucky hat.
Got it at the Citrus Bowl.
It's now got lots of auto-
graphs — Pat Summitt,
Peyton Manning,
Congressman Duncan and
Archie Manning. A little
girl I didn't know wanted
to sign it, so she did. It
says Mary C. Just lots of
interesting people."*

Governor Don Sundquist

Nashville, Tennessee

"I haven't seen too many people wear hair like this, so I thought I'd be original. I've been a Vol fan since birth. Never liked anybody else. When I can't be at the games I'm at home watching them on TV. I've taped every game."

Jason Thomas
Wartrace, Tennessee

GATOR TRAITORS

"The fun about living in
Ocala is being a thorn in
the side of the Gators."
Ron Butler

Karen, Ron and

Kristin Butler

Ocala, Florida

"One of the best moments I've had with the Pride of The Southland Band was at the Orange Bowl. I took my bus down there and it just so happened that we parked right beside the band buses. There we were, me and 15 of my best friends on top of my tour bus right next to the band. So I talked them in to surrounding my bus and playing "Rocky Top." The first time they played "Rocky Top" on January 2, 1998 was for me, personally.

Kenny Chesney
Gallatin, Tennessee

Photo: Kenny Chesney

A BETTER VIEW

A willing Dad comes

through in the clutch.

COMING HOME

"When the Vols run
through the "T", it's like
running through it all over
again for me. It's a unique
feeling...really special.
What makes it so great is
the fans and the people in
the area. That's why I
chose to live back in the
Tennessee area again."

Heath Shuler
1993 Player of the Year

PEYTON WHO?

Sideline somersaults on

Saturday...someday.

Payton Dotson

Nashville, Tennessee

IT'S ALWAYS FOOTBALL TIME IN TENNESSEE

An Orange and White spring game, the perennial pre-season hype, eleven regular season games and a bowl game is enough to quench most Vol fans' thirsts for UT football.

Most, not all.

The fact is, leaving Neyland Stadium for the last time in November is where some Volmaniacs' true obsession begins. Actual turf in a den, opposing team stickers in toilets, the UT logo burned into china, and an actual 'T' as a home entrance.

Crazy? Possibly.

Volmaniac? Definitely.

Greg and Sally Langley and Sally's twin sister, Sandy are serious about their Volunteers. Just look inside the Langley House of Orange. Nearly every square inch is covered with something orange, something UT, something Volunteer. Even the carpet in their den is the 30-yard line from Neyland Stadium's old artificial turf. "I love coming home," says Sally. Each day I am so happy. I mean, how could you possibly be in a bad mood when surrounded by all this orange?"

L to R: Sandy Troope, Greg and Sally Langley Nashville, Tennessee

CONSTANT REMINDER

Even at the office, Greg
Langley surrounds himself
with his favorite pastime.

VU PU & BAMA 2

Langley bathroom

Nashville, Tennessee

HOME IS WHERE THE ORANGE IS

Greg and Sally Langley's
bedroom
Nashville, Tennessee

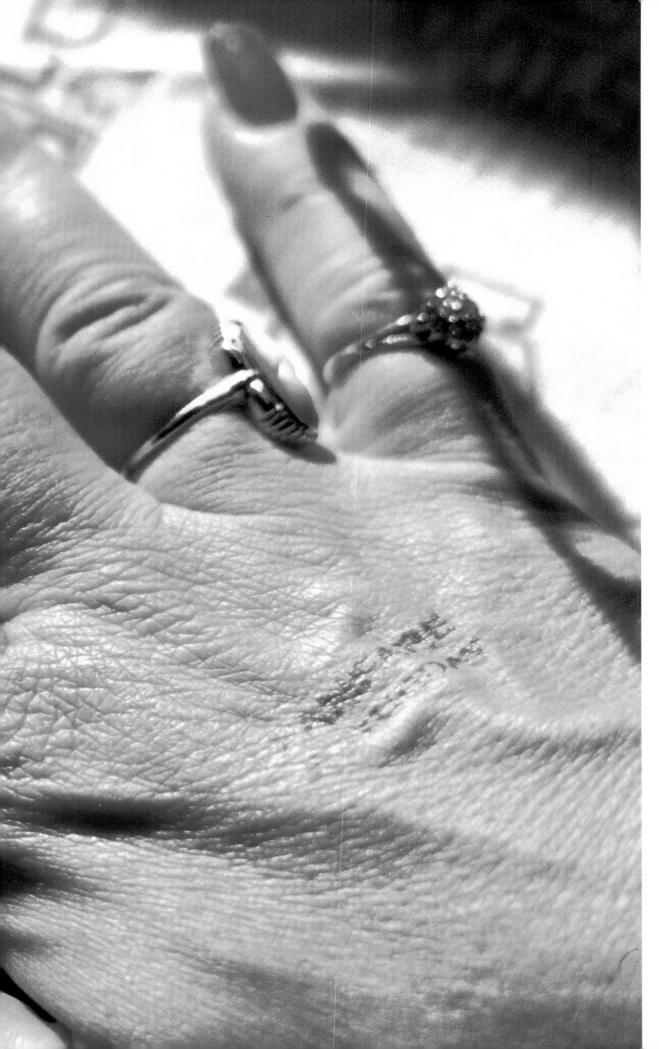

VOLUNTEER VOWS

"We bought these rings at the first Citrus Bowl we went to. A guy had the UT already made so we asked him to make the VOLS. And we wear them every game. If we forget, we go all the way back to the motor home and put them on. We never forget."

Frank and
Carol Armstrong
Columbia, Tennessee

LIKE FATHER, LIKE SON?

*"It's really important to
have all of the fans at the
games. When I'd go down
the Vol Walk, I would look
for the same people every
week. They generally
stand in the same place,
so I'd look for them. And
that support was
important. We would rely
on the crowd to generate
momentum."*

*"I want him to be whatev-
er he wants to be.'*

Stephen and Bubba Miller
(1991-1995,
All SEC 1995)
Nashville, Tennessee

"We have the two largest UT retail stores in Tennessee as well as the largest web site in the world with over 700 pages of merchandise. Our most unusual thing? Women's lingerie."

— David Singleton with wife, Nicole

Tennessee Sports Fan, Nashville, Tennessee

111

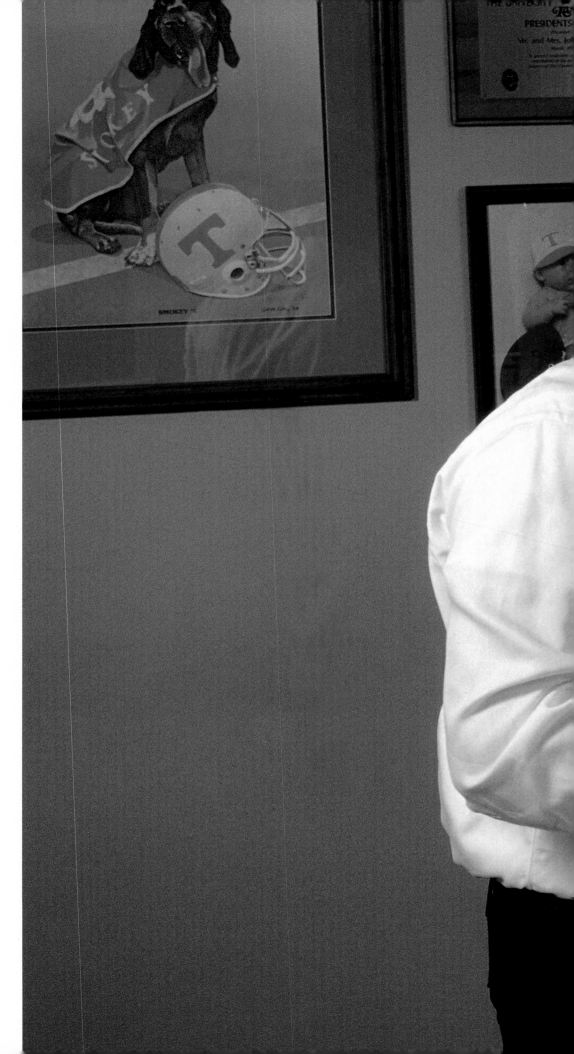

TILL DEATH
DO US PART

"We were watching the '91 Florida game on TV and my wife disappears. At half-time I go check on her, and she's laying on the floor, broke out in a sweat. She's had a gall bladder attack. And so I say, 'Guys, I have to take Karen to the emergency room.'

Nobody gets up, Nobody moves. They sort-of mumble over their shoulders, 'Karen, y'all right?' and then go back to the game. So we get to the ER, my wife is doubled over in pain and I walk over to the television and change the station to watch the game as she is near death. It was so serious she had to have her gall bladder removed. But I got to see the rest of the game."

John Pratt

Franklin, Tennessee

BIG ORANGE COUNTRY

"The reason I'm a fan is because I grew up on Tennessee football from as long as I can remember. As long as I've been able to walk and wear a shirt, I've been wearing a Tennessee shirt."

Kenny Chesney
Gallatin, Tennessee

GRAND ENTRANCE

Jimmy and Bettie Burcham

enjoy a ride through their

very own "T".

Columbia, Tennessee

BIG ORANGE COVER UP

Bettie shows off her hand-
made quilt, a gift from
Nadine Sawyer of
Summertown, TN.

'T' IT UP

The annual Spring
pilgrimage of the Big
Orange Caravan is a
time for camaraderie
that lets UT fans get
together to swap
stories and hang out
with the coaches
when they're not
worrying about their
own game.

Left to right:
Mike Hamilton,
Mike Young,
Tom Cunningham,
Phil Fulmer, and
Johnny Peay

A TALL ORDER

"At the time, our station had been the voice of the Vols for over 20 years. I had seen the LSU game and watched people throw cups and stuff at the players after they lost and saw behavior did not make me proud to be a Vols fan. So I said to my boss that I thought we needed to show our support by having somebody suffer public hardship with them until they won a game. I had no idea that five hours later he would page me to tell me I would be going upon a billboard the next morning.

I was up there 33 days. I ate, slept, did everything up there but shower and go to the bathroom — I did both my shows each day broadcasting live from the billboard. I'm a sleepwalker so I had to tie a rope around me at night so I wouldn't walk off...it was a 40-foot drop! There was rain, lightening, heat and cold. At the beginning there were 90-degree days but at the end I was doing my morning sports in 28-degree weather.

After it was over, they brought me to Knoxville and honored me at the Boston College game with my own jersey with the number 33 for the number of days I spent on the billboard. What's neat about that is two years later James "Little Man" Stewart came to UT to play and he was number 33.

Was it worth it? Yeah, it was. Everybody wants to have something unique about his or her life and I guess I do."

Duncan Stewart
Nashville, Tennessee

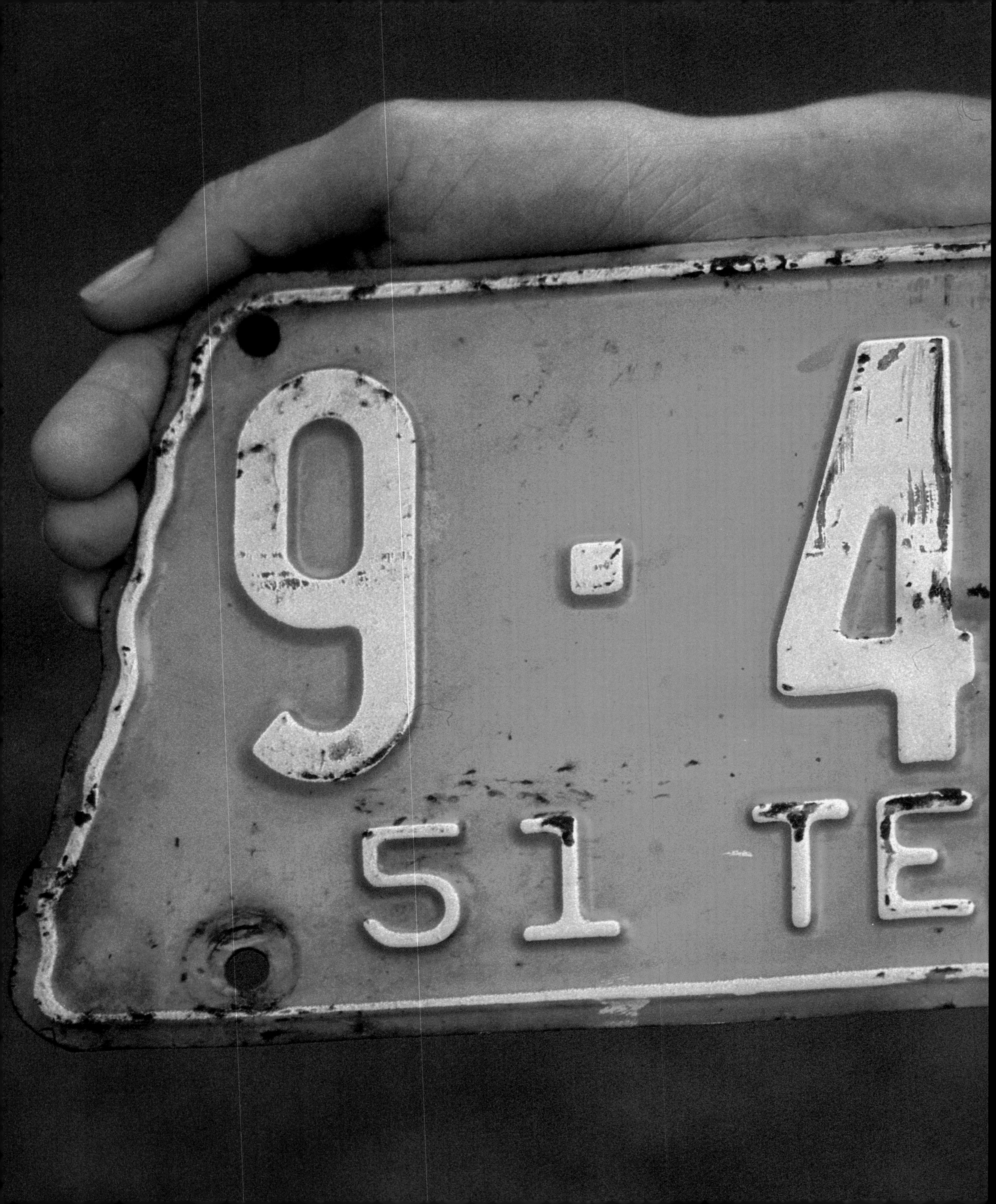
9-4
51 TE

"I like anything with General Neyland on it, that's my thing," says Sullivan. Pieces in his collection include an original 1951 Cotton Bowl game day program, a piece of the 1985 championship goal post, an original picture from the most famous play in Tennessee football history — Johnny Butler's 1939 run against Alabama, Neyland's autograph, and "lots of stuff that nobody else has.

I proposed at the 1986 Alabama game. Then at my wedding, my wife Regina painted an orange UT on her finger so I'd see it when I slipped on her ring. My friend John surprised me and had "Rocky Top" played for our recessional. I guess you could call me a pretty big fan."

Mike Sullivan

College Grove,

Tennessee

JUST A-SWINGIN'

"I get so wrapped up in the spirit. Plus, I don't have anything to talk about at work on Monday if I don't know what happened Saturday at the game."
— Glenda Acree

Les and Glenda Acree
Knoxville, Tennessee

127

CHISLED IN STONE

"The dog that modeled for the sulpture was named Radio. I told him if he sat for me, I would make him famous."

Jennifer Grisham, sculptor

Columbia, Tennessee

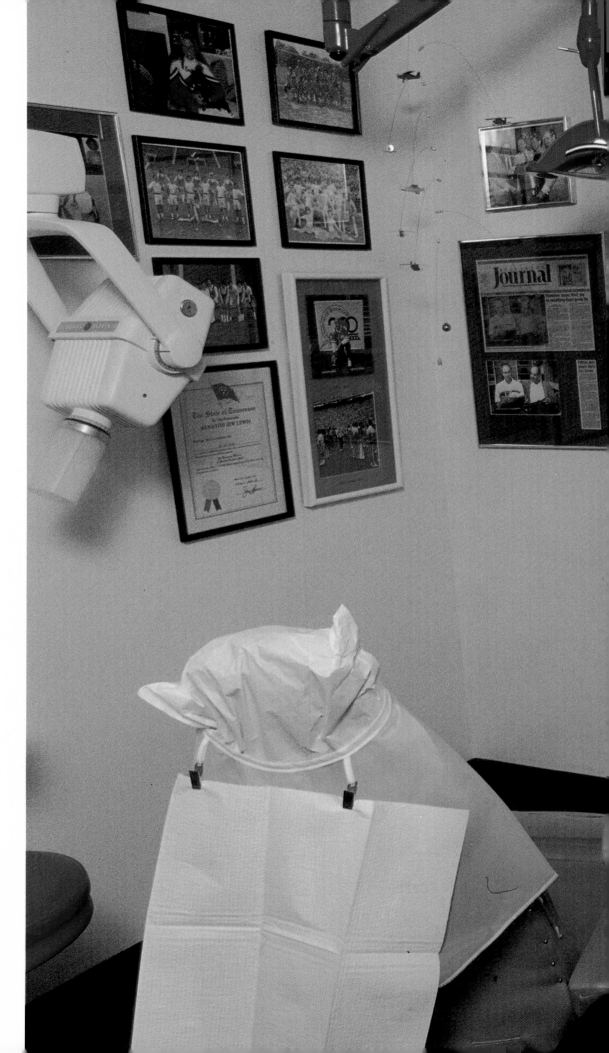

DDS-4-UT

"The memories of UT are priceless to me. That's what makes this whole "mania" concept so important. If you look at all the other SEC schools, we've only won two or three championships for a long time, but yet UT could sell 100,000 seats tomorrow playing North Texas State. It's all because of the background, the memories and the way that the school understands that even though academics are at the heart of a university, the fans are at the soul. Fans and memories make a weekend last a lifetime."

Dr. Jack Fletcher
Nashville, Tennessee
UT cheerleader 1966-1968

Shoes owned and
modeled by
David Dickerson, DDS,
Nashville, Tennessee

Orange Anne
(Jessica) White
Nashville, Tennessee

THE THREE S'S:
BIG ORANGE STYLE

A look inside a Big
Orange fan's bathroom
Nashville, Tennessee

BEAMIN' ORANGE

"If you cut me, I bleed orange. I'm a big football fan, but only Tennessee football. I don't care much for other teams. If they don't wear orange, I don't watch."

Lee Beaman with daughters Katherine (left) and Natalie

Nashville, Tennessee

FAN FARE

"I wear three buttons
every day — Coach
Fulmer, Peyton Manning
and Alan Jackson.
I've only been to one game
in Knoxville but I watch
every game on TV.
I scream like they could
hear me. My favorite
thing was getting to meet
Peyton Manning. I said
'Oh, Lord, I'm standing
beside Peyton Manning.'
I couldn't believe it. I was
going to talk to him but
I went blank. All I could
say was 'take care.'"

Margie Lokey
Nashville, Tennessee

SMALL VOL

"We brought her home from the hospital in an orange and white UT suit and they've been her favorite colors ever since," says mom, Connie Watson of 8-month-old daughter, Taylor."

Taylor Watson

Murfreesboro,

Tennessee

143

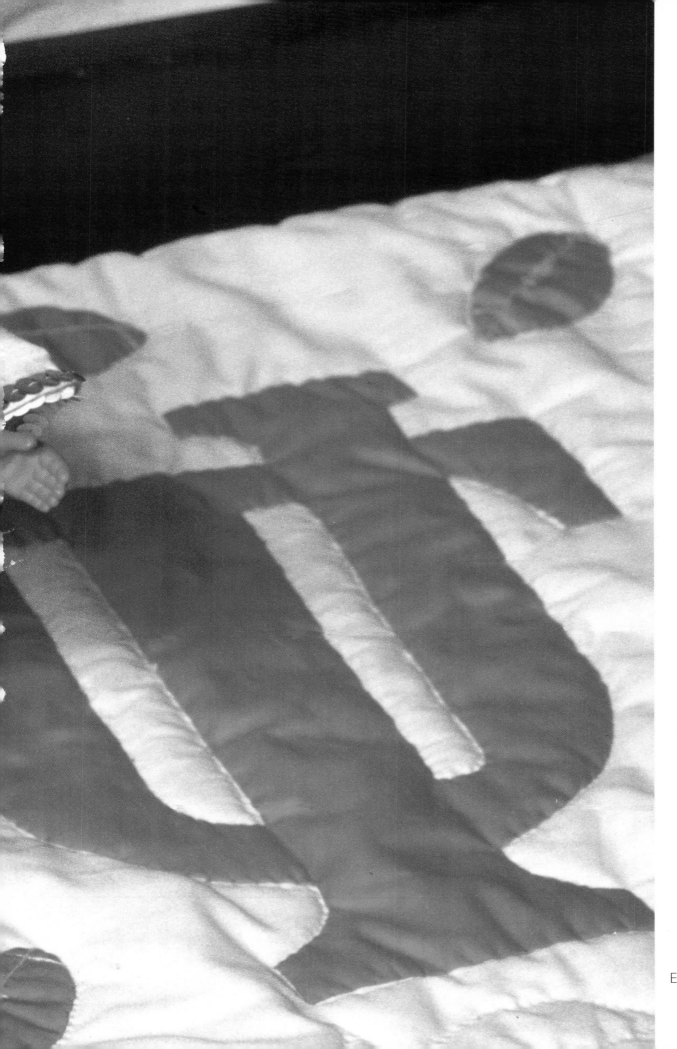

ELVIS WAS A UT FAN

SUMMER KICKOFF

John Ward addresses a
crowd of friends and fans at
The Davidson County
Alumni Chapter's annual
UT picnic at Nashville's
National Guard Armory.

MEETING THE MAN

Debbie Burns of New
Johnsonville, Tennessee,
meets Coach Fulmer at the
Davidson County annual
picnic.

*The last game we missed
was in November 1987,
because I had a heart
attack. It was a
Wednesday and at the
hospital I sat up in bed
and said: 'Doc, you think
you can get me out of here
by Saturday?...I didn't
want to miss the
Mississippi homecoming.
He said 'no way' so I
missed that one and the
Kentucky game. The doc-
tor told me not to go to the
Vanderbilt game but I
went anyway. If my
memory serves me
correctly, at half time they
were up about 23 to 6 and
Darlene thought I was
going to have another
attack...but we came back
and won it.*
— Larry Eley

Larry and
Darlene Eley
Franklin, Tennessee

Vol Claus

"I started dressing up as Santa Claus four years ago. At first it was just a red suit, but two years ago I decided I needed an orange one, so my mother and I got together and she made it. I call him Vol Claus and only wear it one time a year — to the Vandy game. Everybody gets a kick out of it. The people that sit next to us had their picture taken with me and used it for their Christmas card."
— Joe York,
Ashland City, Tennessee

REST ASSURED

Two life-altering things
are getting married and
death, and both can be
celebrated in UT style.
Here, John and Louella
McElroy of Knoxville,
Tennessee were surprised
when, after reciting their
wedding vows, they
turned around to greet
their guests and found
each waving an orange
and white pom-pom.

155

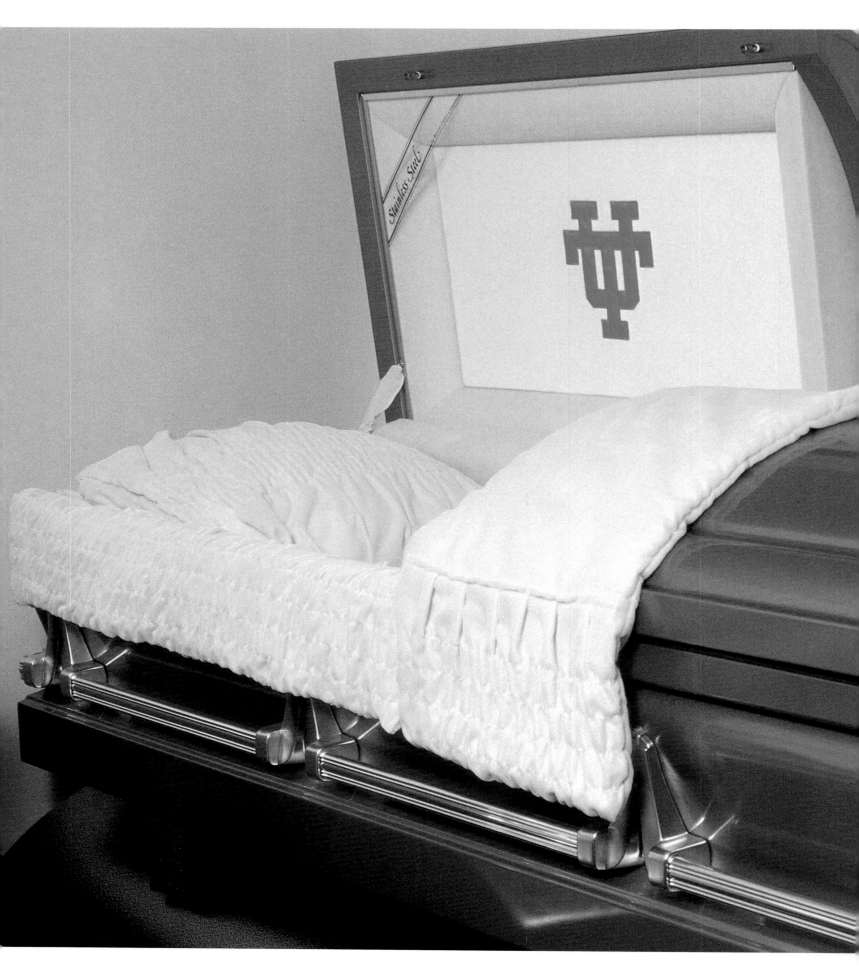

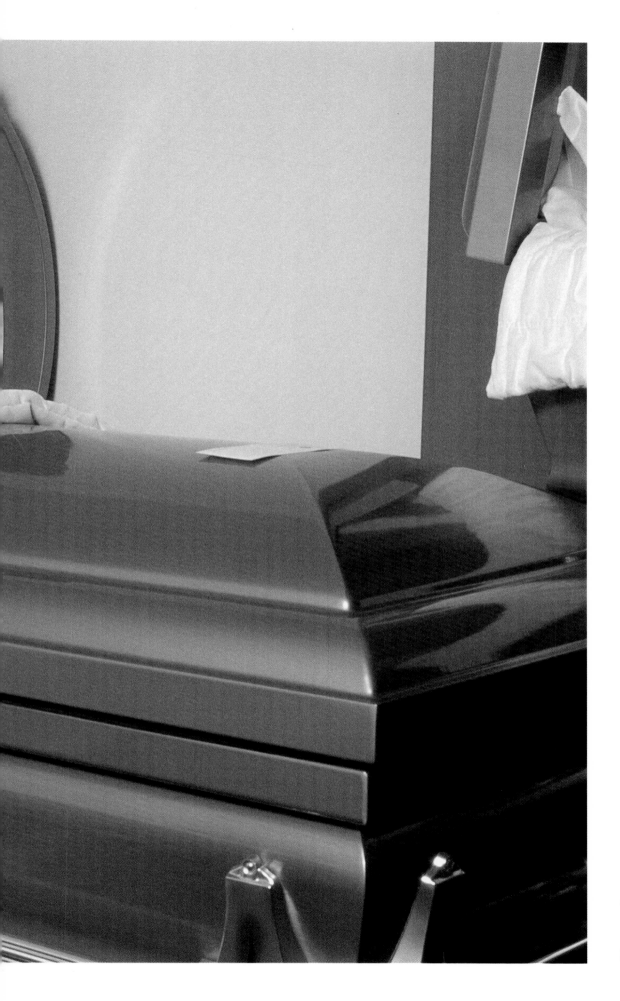

THE VOICE

"The strength of the Vol Network is the people who listen. Like the young man who maybe four or five years ago called our telephone talk show and introduced himself from Newberger Tennessee. He talked about his experiences, how he loved the university, how he lived for Tennessee football and basketball games. And as we were about to hang up he said, "I want to tell you. I'm 24 now, but when I was just a youngster, a little seven year old boy in the back yard, I was in an accident. A tree limb hit me right between the eyes and since that happened I've been blind. But I want to tell you Mr. Ward, that when I listen to the broadcast, I can see the game.'

The strength of the Vol Network is not in an announcer who talks. Now and for years and years to come, rest assured, the strength of the Vol Network is the people who listen. The people who listen. Like you."

—John Ward